# design motifs

# design motifs of

# ancient mexico

## Jorge Enciso

DOVER PUBLICATIONS, INC., NEW YORK

*Design Motifs of Ancient Mexico* is a new unabridged English translation of the work originally published in 1947 under the title *Sellos del Antiguo Mexico*.

*Standard Book Number: 486-20084-1*

*Library of Congress Catalog Card Number: 53-13273*

Manufactured in the United States of America
Dover Publications, Inc.
180 Varick Street
New York, N. Y. 10014

# acknowledgments

I am deeply indebted to Francisco S. Iturbe. I place his name first on this list because it was through his generous supervision that this book was made possible.

I am grateful to the ancient National Museum from whose collection I chose the best examples of seals for this selection; the Directors: Dr. Alfonso Caso, Professor Eduardo Noguera and Dr. Daniel F. Rubin de la Borbolla; the Professors: Jose Garcia Payon, Juan Valenzuela, Roberto J. Weitlaner, Alfonso Ortega, and the artist Miguel Covarrubias whose collections and skill have been very helpful.

I have also included designs of seals from the Museums of Teotihuacan and Chiapas, and from the collections of Diego Rivera and Roberto Montenegro, Angel Rodriguez, William Spratling, Agustin Gomez y Gutierrez, Dr. Artemio Jacome of Zempoala, Veracruz, Eduardo Mead, Jorge Hauswaldt, Helmuth Franck, Kurt Schleu, B. Meneses, Raul Dehesa, Demetrio Garcia, Guillermo Echaniz, Luis Orellano, — all of whom have collaborated enthusiastically to make this selection possible.

J. E.

This edition is dedicated

to the memory of the author

**Jorge Enciso**

who died 30 March 1969.

# preliminary note

## 1 the purpose of the publication

This book is not intended as a scientific dissertation nor as an historical study of stamps. It is a display of native decorative ingenuity which, ancient as it may be, is none the less new to us. The artistic imagination which conceived and executed this manifestation of beauty has left an invaluable source which will, no doubt, serve as an inspiration for our modern plastic arts.

# 2 selection

None of the traces left of the old indigenous cultures of Mexico has attracted my curiosity as much as the small baked clay objects called stamps. Their variety and ingenuity interested me intensely.

By stretching a thin sheet of paper over the stamp and by retracing the surface with a pencil, it was simple to secure an exact reproduction of the decorative motifs; a little retouching, where depressions or imperfections blotted the original design, completed the exact reproduction of the actual decoration. The accumulation of drawings brought out the wide range of motifs and techniques, their numerous applications, and the extent of their geographical provenance.

# 3 raw materials

Stamps were generally made of baked clay. Occasionally, one finds the use of other materials, as the two stone samples from Yucatan, one of copper from Patzcuaro, and another made of bone from Xochimilco. It is evident that stone was not a favorite choice of material for this kind of implement. If any gold or silver was used, the stamps have yet to be found or have been melted long ago. Wood and bone have not survived the ravages of time. This may explain the abundant survival of clay stamps.

# 4 techniques of manufacture

In ancient Mexico, the oldest clay stamps were hand modeled. The increasing demand led to the introduction of a new technique, the mold-made stamp, for mass production.

Pliable clays, to which a proper tempering was added, were used for this purpose. One can often recognize quartz-like sand in the composition. The mixture was sifted and ground, the proper amount of water was added, and the emulsion was left to set for some time until fermentation began. Finally the material was ready for hand modeling or mold production. Baking was done in primitive kilns, heated by wood, somewhat similar to those still in use by the modern potters.

# 5 forms

The shape is indicative of its use. Flat and cylindrical forms were used for stamping flat surfaces; concave for convex surfaces, and vice versa.

With the exception of cylindrical stamps, other forms have handles, flat, conical, basket-like, or rattle-shaped. Cylindrical stamps have a lengthwise hole through which a stick was introduced. The device served as an axis which allowed the stamps to turn on the surface on which the design was to be made. Some have grooves on the ends for rolling with two fingers. Others are rolling-pin shape to be used with both hands.

# 6 reproduction

The stamping process was frequently used to decorate pottery. It was applied to the surface of the vessel when the clay was still pliable. The result was a decoration in relief. Pottery from San Anton, in Cuernavaca, is a good example of the use of this technique today. Sometimes the stamps were used as a mold to make the whole vessel with its decorations.

Skin, cloth or paper were printed by applying a previously inked stamp. The Indians were familiar with a great variety of vegetable and mineral dyes. Some of the most commonly used for stamping were: smoke black from pine trees, a black soil, Ocotl, Tlayacac, or pine charcoal for black; white soil or chalk,, Tizatlali, and gypsum. Chimaltizatl for white; Achiotl, cochineal, Nochistli, and the sap of the Escuahuitl, the tree of blood, for red; Tecozahuitl, yellow soil, the sap of argemone, 'thorny poppy,' and the Zacatlascal, a parasite of certain tropical trees for yellow; indigo for blue; indigo mixed with white and alum for turquoise blue. Colors were well ground and then mixed with oil of chia, Mexican argemone, or alum, Tlalxocotl. Printed patterns were rectangular, circular, elliptical, triangular, or irregular, depending on their various ornamental uses. Prints made by cylindrical stamps have two parallel lines running lengthwise which served as marginal guides in the printing of sashes and belts.

# 7 sizes

The size varies according to the surface space to be decorated. The smallest stamp known measures one square centimeter; the largest, a cylindrical specimen from Tlatilco, 23 centimeters in length.


# 8 geographical distribution

It must be mentioned that stamps were articles of trade; thus, the places where they are found today are not necessarily their places of origin. For the purposes of this publication, we shall consider only the localities where they have been found.

In the United States, stamps have been discovered in Indiana, Illinois, Arizona, Ohio, Michigan, New Mexico and Florida.

In Mexico, they are found principally on the high central plateau in the State of Guerrero and on the Gulf of Mexico. They are scarce on the Pacific lowlands, the Isthmus of Tehuantepec, the peninsula of Yucatan, and southern Mexico.

They are known in the Antilles, Puerto Rico, among the Taino Indians, in the Central American countries, and in Colombia among the Quimbaya Indians, to the west of Cauca River. Samples from this locality are known to be made of stone and sheet gold. In Ecuador, Brazil, and on the shores of the Negro River, wooden stamps are used. North of Trujillo, in Peru, gourds were carved to be used as stamps.

# 9 chronology

It is a well known fact that stamps were in use in ancient Mediterranean cultures. Nevertheless, no evidence suggests importation from the Old World. Stratigraphic research has shown that stamps in the New World have been in use since ancient times. Tlaltilco, Los Remedios, La Venta, etc., offer eloquent evidence of this statement. Stamps appear among the Mayas although only rarely in the Old Empire. They are found in Teotihuacan and in Monte Alban. They were very popular among the Olmecs, Teotihuacanans, Totonacs, and Nahuas. After the conquest, their use was restricted to the printing of trademarks, pottery, popular confectionary, and in some places, identification.

Geometric design was common in the oldest stamps in spite of its abstract character. The apparent explanation for this trait is that the design is easily made. There followed naturalistic designs, plants, flowers, animals, and human figures, to be combined finally with geometric designs. Naturalistic motifs became so simplified that they eventually appeared as conventional symbols, stepped-frets, etc. Lastly, fantastic patterns were created using the former elements: symbolic, ceremonial, or artificial figures, taken from other native crafts, rites, or customs.

In the present publication, an attempt has been made to arrange the plates by subject matter rather than by cultural or chronological groups. F. S. Meyer's classification, as shown by his 'Manual de Ornamentacion' has been followed. This in turn follows the principles laid down by Semper, Boticher and Jacobsthal.

NOTE: The stamps shown in the following plates are all in private collections unless otherwise specified in the captions.

Pottery bowl from San Miguel Amantla, D. F. The decorations were stamped. Publications of the American International School of Archaeology and Ethnology. Mexico, 1911-1912.

Fragments of Codex Chalchihuitzin Vazquez, from San Salvador Zampango, Tlaxcala. The American Museum of Natural History, New York. Middle of the 16th Century. The decorations seen on the arms of the figure made with stamps.

Flat clay stamp from the State of Veracruz.

Flat stamp from the state of Michoacan.

Convex stamp from Mexico City.

Cylindrical stamp from the State of Veracruz.

Bone stamp from Xochimilco, D. F.

# contents

## Geometric Motifs

Zigzags . . . . . . . . . . . . . . . . . . . . . . . . Plates 1 and 2

Triangles . . . . . . . . . . . . . . . . . . . . . . . . 3 and 4

Squares . . . . . . . . . . . . . . . . . . . . . . . . 5 to 9

Circles . . . . . . . . . . . . . . . . . . . . . . . . 10 to 12

Spirals . . . . . . . . . . . . . . . . . . . . . . . . 13 to 17

Steps . . . . . . . . . . . . . . . . . . . . . . . . 18 to 20

Stepped-fret patterns . . . . . . . . . . . . . . . . . . . 21 to 32

Crosses . . . . . . . . . . . . . . . . . . . . . . . . 33

Various geometric motifs . . . . . . . . . . . . . . . 34 to 41

# Natural Forms - Flora

Flowers . . . . . . . . . . . . . . . . . . . . 42 to 52

Vegetables . . . . . . . . . . . . . . . . . . 53 to 54

Blue worm . . . . . . . . . . . . . . . . . . 55 to 60

Shells . . . . . . . . . . . . . . . . . . . . . 61 to 62

Spiders and various insects . . . . . . . . 63

Butterflies . . . . . . . . . . . . . . . . . . 64 to 66

Fishes . . . . . . . . . . . . . . . . . . . . . 67

Toads, frogs . . . . . . . . . . . . . . . . . 68

Lizards . . . . . . . . . . . . . . . . . . . . 69 to 70

Serpents . . . . . . . . . . . . . . . . . . . 71 to 74

Plumed serpents . . . . . . . . . . . . . . 75 to 77

Fire serpents . . . . . . . . . . . . . . . . . 78 to 81

Flint serpents . . . . . . . . . . . . . . . . 82

Fantastic serpents . . . . . . . . . . . . . 83

Alligators . . . . . . . . . . . . . . . . . . . 84

Buzzards . . . . . . . . . . . . . . . . . . . 85

Owls . . . . . . . . . . . . . . . . . . . . . . 86

Eagles . . . . . . . . . . . . . . . . . . . . . 87 to 89

Humming-birds . . . . . . . . . . . . . . . 90

Pheasants . . . . . . . . . . . . . . . . . . 91 to 92

Aquatic birds . . . . . . . . . . . . . . . . 93

Quetzals . . . . . . . . . . . . . . . . . . . 94

Various unidentified birds . . . . . . . . 95 to 100

Fantastic birds . . . . . . . . . . . . . . . . . 101 to 103

Deer . . . . . . . . . . . . . . . . . . . . . . 104

Dogs, wolves (coyotes) . . . . . . . . . . . . . 105 to 109

Jaguars, pumas . . . . . . . . . . . . . . . . 110 to 112

Various and unidentified mammals . . . . . . . 113 to 114

Monkeys . . . . . . . . . . . . . . . . . . . . 115 to 122

Fantastic animals . . . . . . . . . . . . . . . 123 to 125

# The Human Body

Human figures . . . . . . . . . . . . . . . . . 126 to 128

Heads and masks . . . . . . . . . . . . . . . . 129 to 131

Masks of deities . . . . . . . . . . . . . . . . 132

Skulls . . . . . . . . . . . . . . . . . . . . . 133

Hands . . . . . . . . . . . . . . . . . . . . . 134

Fantastic human figures . . . . . . . . . . . . 135 to 138

# Artificial Forms

Twists and braids . . . . . . . . . . . . . . . 139 to 140

Rattles . . . . . . . . . . . . . . . . . . . . 141 to 143

'Patolli' . . . . . . . . . . . . . . . . . . . . 144

Movement . . . . . . . . . . . . . . . . . . . 145 to 146

Decorations related to architecture . . . . . . 147 to 148

Trophies . . . . . . . . . . . . . . . . . . . . 149 to 150

Emblems . . . . . . . . . . . . . . . . . . . . 151 to 152

Decorations of chronological significance . . . 153

# plates

# geometric motifs

Cylindrical stamps decorated with zigzag motifs. I is from Colima, II and III are from the State of Mexico.

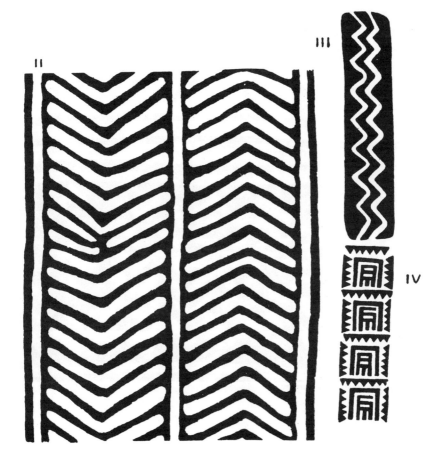

I is a flat stamp showing representation of the fire serpent or solar ray (?). II is a cylindrical stamp from Las Tunas, Colima. III is a flat stamp from Michoacan. IV is a flat stamp found in Azcapotzalco, D.F. All show zigzag motifs.

Stamps showing banded motifs combined with triangles and circles. I and III are from Mexico City. II is from Oaxaca. Collection is in the National Museum of Mexico.

Flat stamps decorated with triangles and parallel lines. I, II, and IV were found in Mexico City. III and V are from Chimalpa, Mexico.

Stamps displaying decoration based on concentric squares. I and III are from
Mexico. II was found in Guerrero.

5

Decoration based on concentric squares. I is a cylindrical stamp from Guerrero. II is a flat stamp found in Mexico City. III is a flat stamp from Huaxcama, San Luis Potosi. IV is a flat stamp found in Mexico City.

**6**

Cylindrical stamps decorated with concentric squares. I is from Mexico. II was found in Puebla.

Cylindrical stamps using angles and quadrilaterals as decorative motifs. I is from Guerrero. II is from Comacalco, Tabasco.

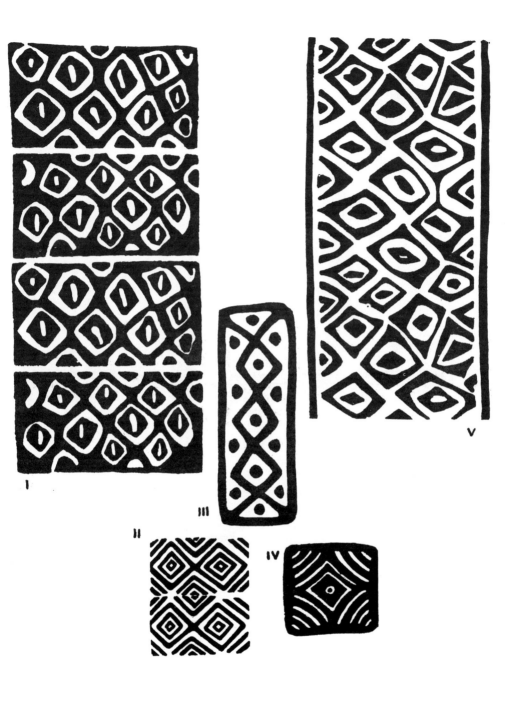

I and V are cylindrical stamps from Veracruz. II and IV are flat stamps from Mexico City. III is a flat stamp from Guerrero. The designs are based on squares.

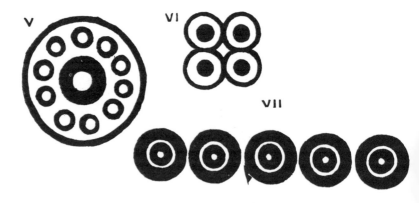

Flat stamps displaying designs based on concentric circles. I, II, III, and IV were found in Mexico City. V is from Tlatelolco. IV and VII were found in Oaxaca.

I is a cylindrical stamp and II is flat. The patterns are a combination of spirals and concentric circles. Both are from Mexico City.

I

II

I is a cylindrical stamp and II is flat. The designs use concentric circles. Both are from Mexico City.

I

II

I is a flat stamp decorated with curvilinear spirals and angles, a variation of the stepped-fret (Xicalcoliuhqui) design. II is a flat stamp with a variation of I. Both are from Mexico City.

I

II

III

Flat stamps showing angular and curved spirals. I is from Azcapotzalco. II was found in Mexico. III is from Tlaxcala.

Flat stamps using curvilinear spirals and angular motifs. I, II, and IV were in Mexico City. V is from Chalco, State of Mexico. III is from Apatzingan.

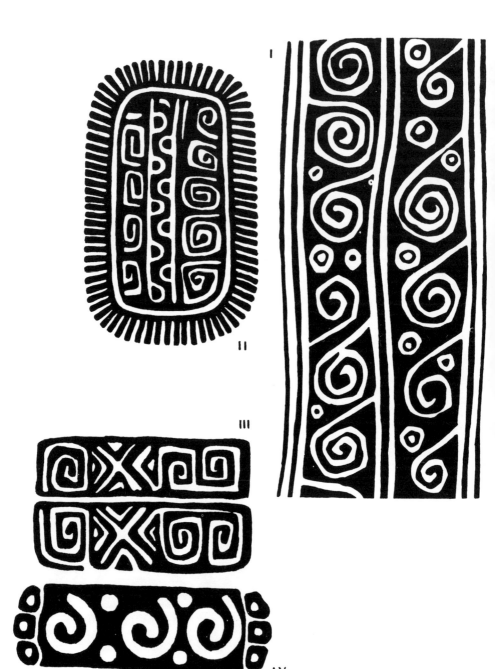

I is a cylindrical stamp from Mexico City. II and III are flat stamps from Morelos, and IV was found in Guerrero. The decoration consists of angular and curved spirals.

**16**

Angular and curved spirals. All are flat forms. I and IV are from Churubusco. II, III, and V are from Guerrero.

Cylindrical stamp using step pattern. I is from Tula, Hidalgo. II shows stepped-fret (Xicalcoliuhqui) pattern and was found at Acolman, Mexico.

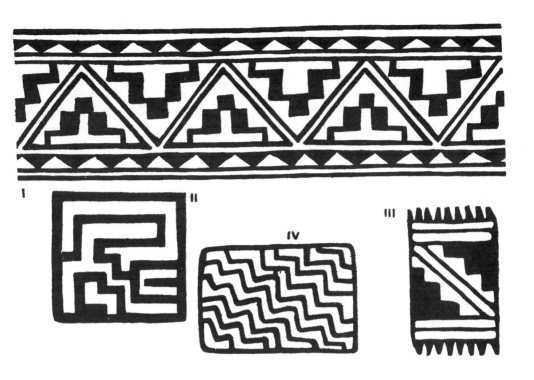

I is a cylindrical stamp found in Mexico City. II and IV are flat stamps from Mexico City. III is a flat stamp from Teotihuacan. V is a flat stamp from Texcoco.

Flat stamps decorated with step motifs. I, II, and III are from Mexico City. IV and V were found at Texcoco.

I is a cylindrical stamp and II is flat. The design was originally used on gourds—
a stepped-fret (Xicalcoliuhqui) design which in this case is combined with the
spiral motif. Both stamps were found in Mexico City.

I is a cylindrical stamp from Oaxaca. II, III, IV, V, and VI are flat stamps. II and III were found in Mexico City. IV, V, and VI, are from Guerrero. The designs show variations of the stepped-fret (Xicalcoliuhqui) pattern.

I and II are cylindrical stamps. III and IV are flat. The decoration is a variation of the stepped-fret (Xicalcoliuhqui) design. All are from Mexico City.

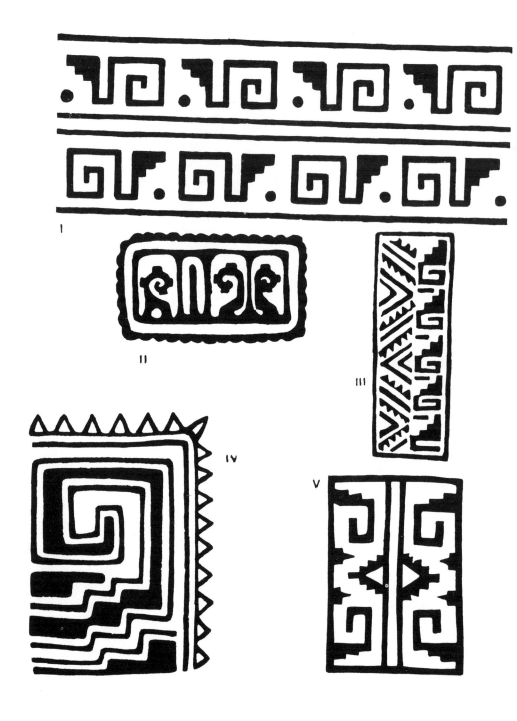

I is a cylindrical stamp from Mexico City. II is a flat stamp from Mexico City. III and IV are flat stamps from Puebla. V is a flat stamp from Guerrero. All are representations of the stepped-fret (Xicalcoliuhqui) pattern.

I, II, III, and IV are flat stamps found in the State of Mexico. V is a cylindrical stamp from Guerrero: All are variations of the stepped-fret (Xicalcoliuhqui) pattern.

Flat stamps showing variations of the stepped-fret (Xicalcoliuhqui) pattern. I, IV, V, VI, and VII are from Mexico City. II, III, and VIII are from Guerrero.

I

II

Flat stamps with the stepped-fret (Xicalcoliuhqui) pattern, a design used originally on gourds. All are from Mexico City. I is in the National Museum of Mexico.

I is a cylindrical stamp from Mexico City. II is a flat stamp from Mexico City. III is a flat stamp from Texcoco. IV is a flat stamp from the State of Mexico. V is a cylindrical stamp from the State of Mexico. All are variations of the stepped-fret (Xicalcoliuhqúi) pattern.

I is a cylindrical stamp from Mexico City. II, III, and IV are flat stamps from Guerrero. V and VI are flat stamps found in Mexico City. All are variations of the stepped-fret (Xicalcoliuhqui) pattern.

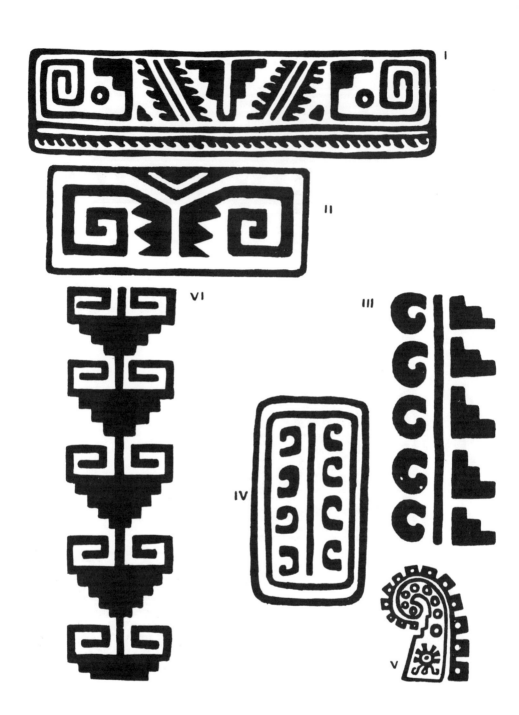

Flat stamps showing representations of steps and hooks, elements and variations of the stepped-fret (Xicalcoliuhqui) pattern. I, II, and VI were found in
Mexico City. III is from Veracruz. IV and V are from Teotihuacan.

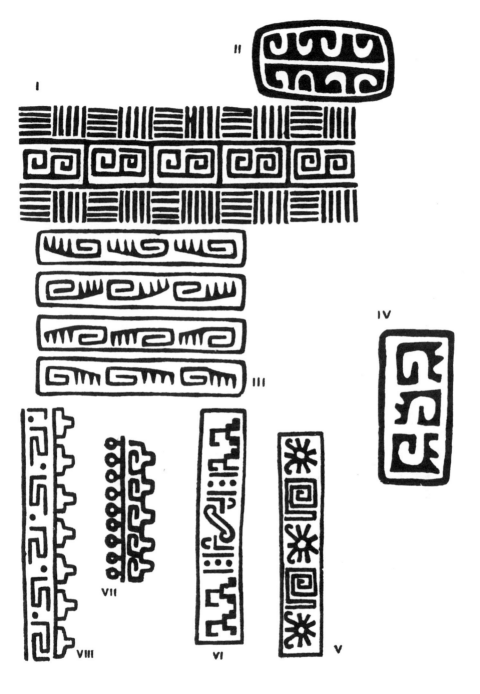

I is a cylindrical stamp from Mexico City. II and IV are flat stamps from Mexico City. III is a flat stamp from Oaxaca. VI, VII, and VIII are flat stamps from Azcapotzalco.

I

II

III

All are cylindrical stamps decorated with hooks and angular spirals taken from the stepped-fret (Xicalcoliuhqui) design. All are from Mexico City.

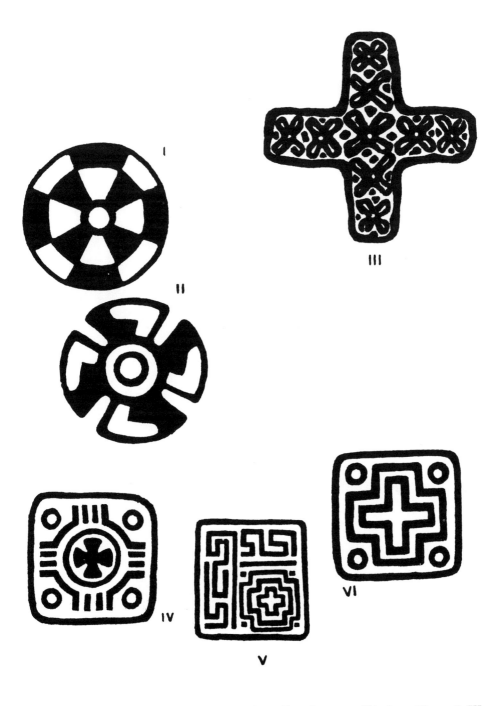

Flat stamps with cruciform patterns. I is from Teotihuacan. II is from Nayarit. III was found in Tres Zapotes, Veracruz. IV is from the State of Puebla. V and VI are from Mexico City.

The crudeness of the different geometric patterns in these flat stamps is indicative of the antiquity of the design. I was found in Chimalpa; II in Tepozotlan, Morelos. III, IV, and VI are from the Valley of Mexico. V is from Tlatilco. VII is from Los Remedios, Mexico.

I is a cylindrical stamp found in Mexico City. II is a flat stamp from the State of Mexico. III is a cylindrical stamp found in Jalisco. The patterns are made up of parallel lines and symmetrical groupings.

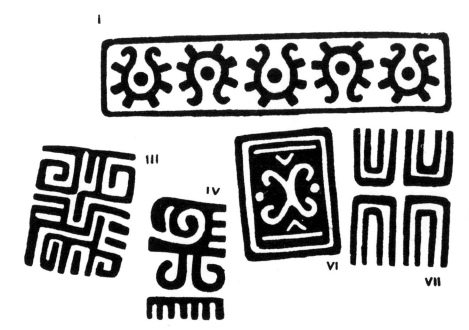

Flat stamps showing patterns using hooks and parallel lines. I, III, IV, VI, and VII were found in Mexico City. II is from Tetelpam, D. F. V is from Tecoloapa, Toluca.

Flat stamps showing decorations using hooks, parallel lines, circles, etc. I, III, IV, and VI were found in Mexico City. II is from Los Tuxtlas, Veracruz. V is from Cuautlamayan, S. L. P.

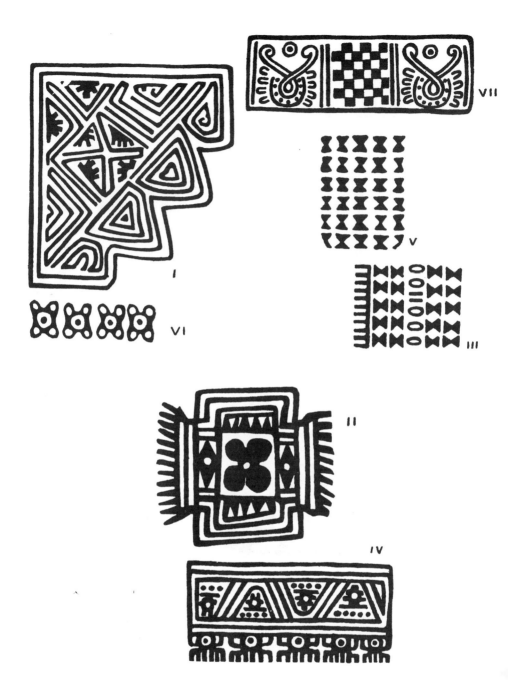

Triangles, concentric circles, and parallel lines used on flat stamps. I and VI are from Mexico City. II and IV were found in Guerrero. III and V are from Chalco, Mexico. VII is from Patzcuaro.

Flat stamps with geometrical designs based on circles, hooks, and dots. I and V are from Mexico City. II was found in Los Tuxtlas, Veracruz. III and IV are from Texcoco.

Cylindrical stamps with geometrical patterns. I and II are from the State of Mexico. III was found in Veracruz.

I and VI are cylindrical stamps from Mexico City. II is a flat stamp from Jalisco. III is a flat stamp from Veracruz. IV is a flat stamp from Mexico City. V is a flat stamp from Chalco, Mexico.

# natural forms
## flora

I uses aquatic flowers as a motif and comes from the State of Mexico. II, with an unidentified motif, comes from Nayarit. III uses aquatic flowers and comes from Xico. IV comes from Puebla. All are flat stamps.

Floral (Xochitl) motifs used on flat stamps. I, III, and VI come from the State of Mexico. II, IV, and VII were found in Azcapotzalco, D. F. V is from Guerrero.

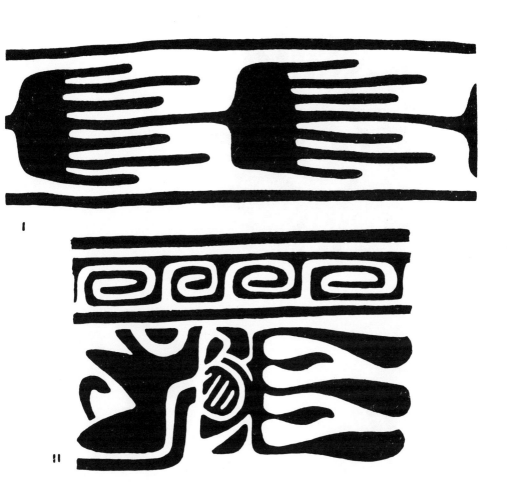

I

II

Cylindrical stamps representing flowers. All were found in Los Remedios, Mexico. II is not complete.

Flat stamps showing floral designs. I and IV were found in Azcapotzalco, D. F. and are now in the National Museum of Mexico. II is from Texcoco, Mexico. III is from El Contador, Mexico.

I is a design representing the earth in bloom. It was found in Mexico City. II, III, and IV utilize various floral motifs and were all found in Azcapotzalco, D. F.

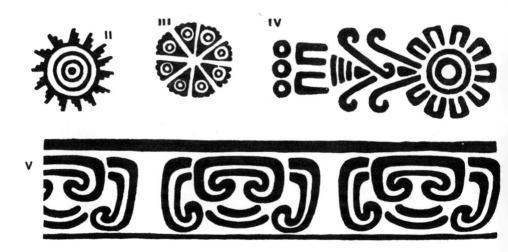

Floral patterns as used in stamps. I is from Ocotlan, Oaxaca and is now in the National Museum of Mexico. II, III, and V are from Mexico City. IV is from Texcoco, Mexico.

Flat stamps showing representations of unidentified flowers. I is from Chalco. II and IV were found in Texcoco. III and VII are from Mexico City. V is from Xico. VI is from Colima.

Flat stamps using floral designs as patterns. I, III, and V are from Mexico City. II and IV were found in Guerrero.

I is a cylindrical stamp from Guerrero displaying a floral (Xochitl) pattern. II is a flat stamp from Veracruz also decorated with a floral design. III is a flat stamp found in Veracruz using an ear of corn as decoration. IV is a flat stamp with a floral design from Mexico City.

Flat stamps of floral designs. I is from Texcoco, Mexico. II, III, IV, VI are from Mexico City. V was found in Tlatilco. VII is from Oaxaca.

Flat stamps with representations of flowers. I, III, and IV are from Mexico City. II was found in Culhuacan, Mexico. V is from Chiauhzingo, Puebla. V I and VII are from Texcoco.

I is a cylindrical stamp with a fern (?) motif from Veracruz. The rest are flat stamps from Mexico City. II and IV show a leaf decoration. III and VII show entwined stems. V represents a knot and VI shows a cactus pattern.

I is a cylindrical stamp from Apatzingan with the representation of vegetables. II is a flat stamp from the State of Mexico and is decorated with leaves. III and VI are flat stamps from Apatzingan and show domesticated plants. IV is a flat stamp from the State of Mexico and shows a potted plant. V is also a flat stamp from the State of Mexico and it uses the cactus motif.

# natural forms
## fauna

Flat stamps showing representations of the blue worm (Xonecuilli), symbol of a constellation or the sceptre of Quetzalcoatl. I is from Guerrero. II is from Morelos. III is from Oaxaca.

I

IV

III

II

V

I is a cylindrical stamp from Mexico City. II is a flat stamp from Texcoco. III and IV are flat stamps from Veracruz. V is a flat stamp from Mexico City. The motif used is that of the blue worm (Xonecuilli).

I is a cylindrical stamp from Mexico City. II, V, and VI are flat stamps from Mexico City. III and IV are flat stamps from Tlaxcala. The blue worm (Xone-cuilli) motif is used in all.

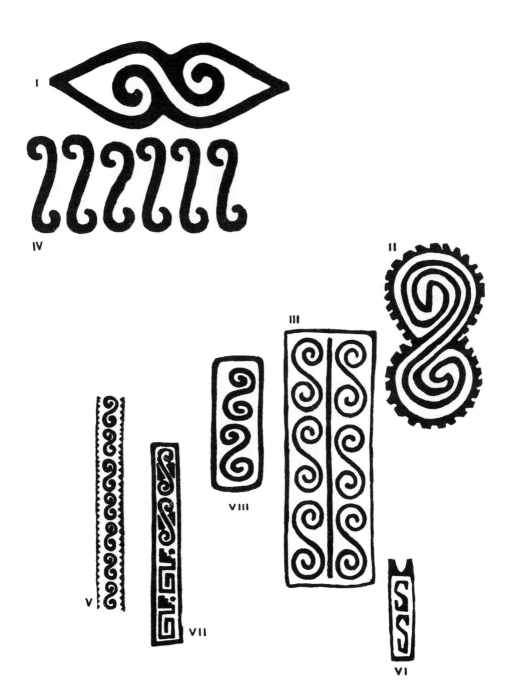

Flat stamps showing representations of the blue worm (Xonecuilli). I, IV, V, VII, and VIII were found in Mexico City. II is from Patzcuaro. III and VI are from Guerrero.

58

Flat stamps showing motifs of the blue worm (Xonecuilli). I, II, IV, and VI are from Mexico City. III, V, and VII were found in Guerrero.

I

II

III

Flat stamps showing variations of the blue worm (Xonecuilli). All were found in the valley of Mexico.

Flat stamps. The cross-section of a sea shell, a design typical of Quetzalcoatl, is the basis of these designs. VI is from Chalco, Mexico. The rest were found in Mexico City.

I is a flat stamp from Mexico City showing a sea shell. II is from Teotihuacan and shows a cross-section of a sea shell. III is a cross-section of a shell and is from Mexico City. IV is a flat stamp showing a cross-section of a shell. V is a flat stamp from Azcapotzalco, D. F. showing a sea shell. VI is a cross-section of a shell from Mexico City. VII is a cylindrical stamp from Mexico City showing a sea shell motif.

I, from Veracruz, has an unidentified pattern. II shows a spider and comes from Veracruz. III and IV are from Veracruz and show insects. V represents a spider and comes from the State of Mexico. The design of VI has not been identified but the stamp is from the State of Mexico. All are flat stamps.

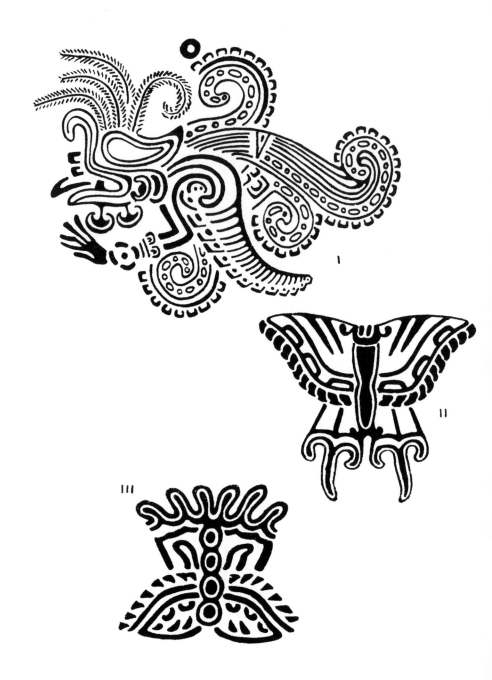

I is a flat stamp from Tula and shows a mythical butterfly (Papalotl). It is now in the National Museum of Mexico. Flat stamps II and III, showing butterflies, were found at Teotihuacan, Mexico.

I is a flat stamp from the National Museum of Mexico and shows a butterfly (Papalotl). II is an incomplete cylindrical stamp from Teotihuacan. III is a flat stamp found in Azcapotzalco, D. F.

Representations of butterflies (Paplotl) on flat stamps. I, III, V, VII, and VIII are from Azcapotzalco II, IV, and VI are from Tlaltelolco.

Flat stamps showing marine life. I is a lobster design found in Veracruz. II is a
fish (Michin) from the State of Tabasco. III, IV, and VI depict fishes and are from
Veracruz. V, from Michoacan, is a representation of a fish.

I and IV are cylindrical stamps showing toads (Tamacolin) and are from Mexico. City. II and III are flat stamps with frog designs and are from Teotihuacan.

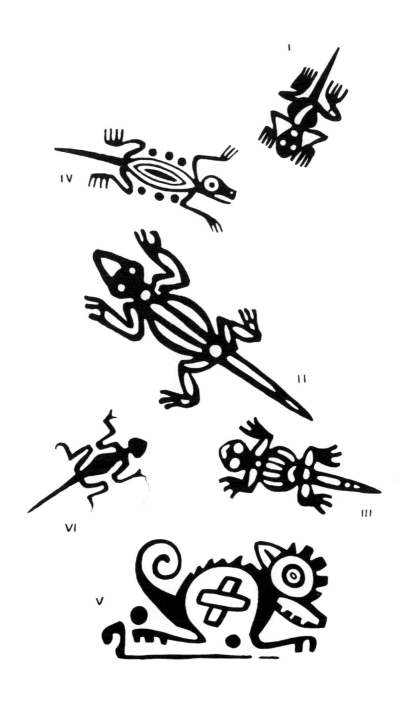

I and IV are lizards (Cuetzpallin) found at Teotihuacan. II and III show lizards and are from Veracruz. V is a Gila monster (Cuautcuetzpallin), from Teotihuacan. VI is a lizard found in Mexico City. All are flat stamps.

Flat stamps showing lizards. I, II, and III are from Texcoco. IV is from Veracruz.
V and VI are from Teotihuacan.

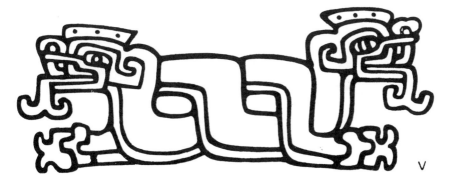

I is a cylindrical stamp found in Piedras Negras, Veracruz. II, III, and IV are flat stamps from Mexico City. V is a flat stamp from Veracruz and is now at the National Museum of Mexico. The motif in all these stamps is a serpent (Coatl) design.

71

I is a cylindrical stamp from Veracruz. II is a flat stamp from Veracruz. III, IV, and V are flat stamps found in Mexico City. The serpent is the motif used in all these stamps.

I is a flat stamp from Azcapotzalco using the serpent as motif. II is a flat stamp from Mexico City showing a serpent's head. III is a flat stamp with a serpent's head found in Coatepec, Toluca.

Stamps using the rattlesnake as a decorative pattern. I is a cylindrical stamp from the State of Guerrero. II is a cylindrical stamp found at Tlatilco, Mexico. III is a flat stamp from Teotihuacan.

Stamps showing representations of the plumed serpent (Quetzalcoatl). I is a cylindrical stamp from the State of Mexico. II is a flat stamp from Tres Zapotes, Veracruz. III is a flat stamp from Michoacan.

Flat stamps showing variations of the plumed serpent design. I and II are from Mexico City, III is from Zamora, Michoacan. IV is from Cempoala, Veracruz.

I is a cylindrical stamp with plumed serpent design found in Mexico City and is now in the National Museum of Mexico. II is a flat stamp showing the plumed serpent design found in Puebla. III is a flat stamp showing a serpent's rattles. It was found in Mexico City and is now in the National Museum of Mexico.

I

II

I is a flat stamp using as a motif the double-headed fire serpent (Xiucoatl) and a wooden rattle (Chicahuastli). II also shows a fire serpent on a flat stamp. Both stamps were found in Mexico City and are now in the National Museum of Mexico.

Stamps decorated with the fire serpent. I is a flat stamp found in Mexico City. II is a flat stamp found in Veracruz. III is a cylindrical stamp from Mexico City. IV and V are flat stamps from the State of Mexico. VI is a flat stamp from Yucatan.

Stamps decorated with the fire serpent. I, V, and VI are flat stamps from Mexico. II is a flat stamp from S. Gregorio, D. F. III is a flat stamp found in Veracruz. IV is a cylindrical stamp from Veracruz. VII is a flat stamp from Texcoco.

Flat stamps with fire serpent motifs. I and V are from the State of Mexico. II is from Mexico City. III, IV, VI, and VII are from Chalco. VIII was found in Guerrero.

Flat stamps showing the flint serpent (Itzcoatl). I and II are from Mexico City. III is from Malinalco, Mexico. All are in the National Museum of Mexico.

Flat stamps decorated with fantastic double-headed serpents. I, III, IV, and V are from Guerrero. II is from Michoacan.

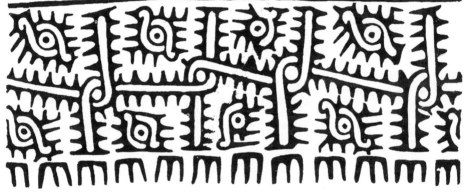

Stamps using the alligator (Cipactli) as motif. I is a cylindrical stamp from Oaxaca. II is a flat stamp from San Andres, Tuxtla. III and IV are flat stamps from Guerrero. V is a flat stamp from Chiapas.

Flat stamps, I and III show buzzards (Tzopilotl) and are from Guerrero. II, IV, and VII represent the king buzzard (Cozcacuautli) and were found in Los Tuxtlas, Veracruz. V and VI represent the king buzzard and were found in Puebla.

Flat stamps. I shows and owl (Tecolotl) found in Teotihuacan. II, showing an owl (Tecolotl), was found in Texcoco. III is an owl head used as a motif and was found in Mexico City. IV is an owl (Tecoltl) design found in Tepoztlan, Morelos.

I

II

Flat stamps with eagle (Cuauhtli) motifs from Mexico City.

I is a cylindrical stamp using both the eagle (Cuauhtli) and the fire serpent (Xiuhcoatl) as motifs. It was found in Azacapotzalco. II is a cylindrical stamp with an eagle motif found in Mexico City. III and V are flat stamps from Mexico City using eagle heads as motifs. IV is a flat stamp from Mexico City using the eagle motif.

Flat stamps, showing motifs of eagles. I, V, and VI were found in the State of Mexico. II, III, and IV are from Mexico City. VII is from Panuco, Veracruz.

Flat stamps. I shows the motif of the hummingbird (Huitzizillin) found in Yucatan. II shows hummingbird and floral designs (Huitziloxochitl) found in Yucatan. III shows hummingbird and flower (Huitziloxochitl) patterns found in Mexico City. IV and V are hummingbird (Huitzizillin) patterns found in Veracruz.

Flat stamps showing motifs of birds' heads (Hueitotollin), ruler for twenty days, commonly called the shouting pheasant (Cojolite, Chachalaca). They are from Veracruz.

All are flat stamps decorated with patterns using the 'road-runner' or 'shouting pheasant.' I is from cempoala, Veracruz. II is from Mexico City. III and IV were found in Veracruz.

Flat stamps with patterns of aquatic fowls. I and III may be San Martin, the kingfisher, and was found in Veracruz. II and IV use herons (Aztatla) as motifs, also from Veracruz. V is a duck (Canauhtli) design found in Mexico City, VI is a heron (Aztatl) motif found in Mexico.

I is a cylindrical stamp from Morelos with a design associated with Quetzalcoatl. II is a flat stamp with quetzal birds (Quetzalli) and was found in Chalco. III repeats the motif, and comes from Santiago Ahuizotla. IV is cylindrically shaped, decorated with the pattern of Quetzalcoatl and was found in Teotihuacan.

**94**

Flat stamps showing motifs of different birds. I shows an owl, II depicts a quail. Both are from Teotihuacan. III and IV represent ducks and are from Chiapas. V represents a macaw and was found in Oaxaca. VI represents a vulture and is from Los Tuxtlas, Veracruz.

Flat stamps. I, II, III, and IV depict unidentified birds at patterns and were all found in the State of Mexico. V shows a feather motif from Colima. VI was found in Guerrero.

Flat stamps showing bird designs. All were found in Mexico City with the exception of III which is from Veracruz.

Stamps displaying various bird patterns. I is a flat stamp from Mexico City. II is a cylindrical stamp from Comacalco, Tabasco. III is from Yucatan.

Flat stamps showing fantastic birds used as decorative motifs. I, III, and VII, the last showing a double-headed bird, were found in Mexico City. II and VI are from Teotihuacan. IV, showing a double-headed bird, and V are from Vera-cruz. VIII uses a double-headed bird as pattern and was found in Calixtlahuaca.

Examples of motifs using fantastic birds as decorative patterns. I, III, IV, using double-headed bird motif, and V are flat stamps from Mexico City. II is a cylindrical stamp found in Veracruz, showing just the head of a bird. VI is a flat stamp from Veracruz. VII is a flat stamp from Xico. VIII is a flat stamp from Teotihuacan, Mexico.

Examples of fantastic birds on flat stamps. I, III, VII, and IX were found in Guerrero. II, VI and VIII were found in Veracruz. IV was found in Culhuacan. V was found in Cuautzingo, Puebla.

Examples of bird patterns on flat stamps. I, III, and V were found in Guerrero II shows a combination of bird and floral designs from Mexico City. IV was found in the State of Veracruz. VI was found in Texcoco, Mexico.

Fantastic bird designs. I and II are flat stamps from Guerrero. III is a flat stamp from Culhuacan, D. F. IV was found in Calixtlahuaca, Mexico. V is a flat stamp from Jalisco. VI is a cylindrical stamp from Tlatilco.

I shows a deer (Mazatl). II shows only head of a deer. Both are flat stamps from Veracruz.

Flat stamps using dog's head (Itzcuintli) as decorative patterns. I and II are from Veracruz. III is from Mexico City.

Flat stamps using dog (Itzcuintli) pattern. I and II are from Veracruz. III is from Comacalco, Tabasco. IV is from Guerrero. V is from Colima.

Flat stamps using dog (Itzcuintli) pattern and are from Veracruz and Cempoala.

Flat stamps using dog (Itzcuintli) pattern from Veracruz.

I is a cylindrical stamp with dog's head (?) found in Yucatan. II is a flat stamp from Mexico City, decorated with an old coyote. III depicts a man wearing a coyote mask. IV is a flat stamp found in Mexico City, showing the coyote flower.

I is a flat stamp showing a jaguar (Ocelotl) and is from Valle Nacional, Oaxaca. Collections of the National Museum in Mexico. II is a variation of I, also from Oaxaca.

I shows a jaguar and serpent motifs from Veracruz. II is a flat stamp showing a tiger's claw and is from Mexico City. III and IV are flat stamps from the Federal District, showing only the ear of a tiger. V is a flat stamp form Veracruz, showing the jaguar motif.

Flat stamps. I shows a puma head (Mixtli) and is from Teotihuacan. II is a jaguar (Ocelotl) found in Puebla. III, showing a puma head (Mixtli), and IV, showing a jaguar, come from Hidalgo.

Flat stamps with a variety of animal and bird motifs. I, IX, and X are skunks (Izquilpatli). II shows a duck, an opossum, and a monkey. III and V are opossums. IV is a badger (Cuauhpezotli). VI and VII are bats (Tzinacantli). IV and VIII are from Veracruz. The rest are from Mexico City.

113

Flat stamps. I has unidentified pattern from Tlatilco. II, III, and V, showing an armadillo (Ayotochtli), are from Veracruz. IV, showing a squirrel (Tlachatotl), is from Puebla. VI, showing a rabbit (Toxtli), is from Teotihuacan.

I is flat stamp depicting a monkey (Ozomatli) God of Dance, the 11th day of the month, and also the emblem of a constellation. It is from Mexico City. II is a cylindrical stamp showing a combination of the monkey, the sun, and the symbol of Tlaloc—from Santiago Ahuizotla.

**115**

I is a cylindrical stamp with monkeys and squirrels as motifs and is from Puebla.
II is a flat stamp with a monkey head as pattern, and is from Teotihuacan.
III is a flat stamp with monkey motif, found in Mexico City.

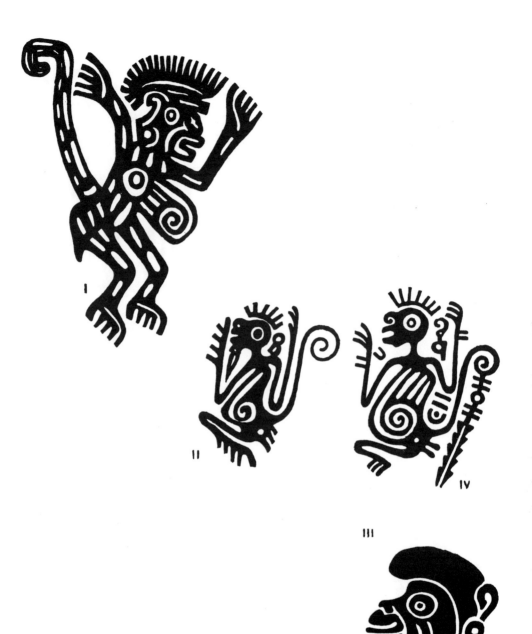

Flat stamps depicting monkey (Ozomatli) patterns. I is from Veracruz. II is
from Puebla. III is from Azcapotzalco. IV is from Texcoco.

All use the monkey (Oxomatli) as motif. I is a flat stamp from Veracruz. II is a cylindrical stamp from Comalcalco, Tabasco. III is a flat stamp from Colima.

Flat stamps depicting the monkey (Ozomatli). I is from Chiapas. II and IV are from Veracruz. III and V are from the Valley of Mexico.

Flat stamps. I uses variation of the Monkey (Ozomatli) pattern, found in Mexico. II and III use a ritual rattle (Chicahuastli) and are from Mexico City. IV and VI use monkey motifs and are from Mexico City. V uses monkey design and is from Veracruz.

All stamps are decorated with monkey (Ozomatli) pattern. I is a cylindrical stamp from Mexico City. II is a flat stamp from Chiapas. III and IV are flat stamps from Mexico. V is from State of Mexico.

Flat stamps depicting monkey or dog and monkey patterns. I shows monkey (Ozomatli) pattern and was found in Veracruz. II depicts dog and monkey motif and is from Guerrero. III shows a monkey and was found in Guerrero. IV is also from Guerrero. V shows a monkey pattern and is from Veracruz.

Fantastic animal patterns. I is a cylindrical stamp from Azoyu. III and IV are flat stamps found in Guerrero. II is a flat stamp from Tlatilco. Collections of the National Museum.

Flat stamps depicting motifs of fantastic animals. I is from Veracruz. II, III, IV, and V are from Guerrero. VI is from Mexico City.

Flat stamps with frets, simplified animals, and geometrical forms. All are from Mexico City.

# the human body

II

I

I is a flat stamp with mythological decoration and was found in Oaxaca. II is a cylindrical stamp found in the state of Mexico and shows an unidentified bird and a human being wearing an animal mask.

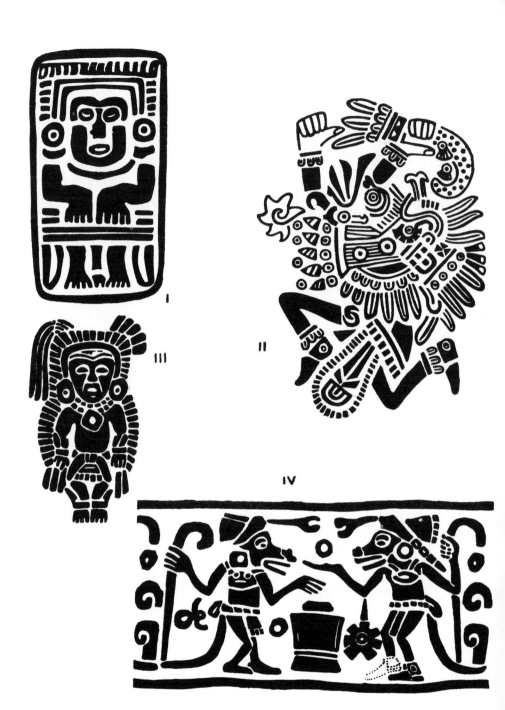

I is a flat stamp from Tampico. II is a flat stamp, depicting Quetzalcoatl, Wind God and plumed serpent, and was found in Texcoco. III is a flat stamp, depicting a masked dancer, from Tlaltelolco. IV is a cylindrical stamp showing human figures, found in the State of San Luis Potesi.

Stamps with human figures. I is a cylindrical stamp from Chalco. II is a flat stamp from Chimalpa. III and VI are flat stamps from Guerrero. IV is a flat stamp from Tlatilco. V is a flat stamp from Chalco.

Stamps with human heads. I is a flat stamp from Oaxaca. II and IV are flat stamps from Azcapotzalco. III is a cylindrical stamp from Veracruz. V is a flat stamp from Mexico City. VI is a flat stamp from Yucatan.

Flat stamps. I shows a head with a large headdress, from Tenayuca. II shows a man and a parrot, from Oaxaca. III shows a mask and is from Veracruz. IV depicts a mask and is from Azcapotzalco. V and VII show heads with large headdresses, from Mexico City.

Flat stamps depicting ritual masks. I and III are from Tlatilco. II is from Los Remedios, Mexico. IV, VI, and VII are from Veracruz. V is from Teotihuacan.

I

II

III

IV

Flat stamps showing masks of deities. I is the Wind God (Ehecatl) and is from Teotahuacan. II is the Rain God (Tlaloc), from Teotihuacan. III shows the Old Man God (Ueueteotl), from Teotihuacan. IV shows the Rain God (Tlaloc) and is from Los Tuxtlas, Veracruz.

Cylindrical stamps. I shows arrowheads and skulls. It is in the National Museum of Mexico. II depicts the man at the place of the dead (Mictlantecutli). Both are from Mexico City.

All use human hands as decoration. I is a cylindrical stamp showing human hands (Maitl), found in Guerrero. II is a flat stamp from Mexico City. III is a flat stamp from Yucatan. IV is a flat stamp from San Andres Tuxtla. V is a flat stamp from Texcoco.

Stamps with fantastic human and animal figures. I is a cylindrical stamp from Guerrero. II is a flat stamp found in Mexico City. III and IV are from Guerrero.

Flat stamps showing fantastic conventionalized designs of human figures and animals. They are all from Guerrero, with the exception of VI which was found in Xochicalco.

Flat stamps depicting fantastic human figures. I is from Chimalpa. II is from Guerrero. III is from Nayarit. IV and V are from Chalco, Mexico.

Flat stamps showing conventional designs of human figures. I and III are from Mexico City. II, V, VI, and VII are from Guerrero. IV is from Jalisco.

# artificial forms

I is a cylindrical stamp showing a cord pattern and is from Comalcalco, Tabasco.
II and III found in Mexico, are variations of the same pattern. IV is a flat stamp
showing another type of cord design, from Texcoco. V is a flat stamp, from
Texcoco, showing interlacing.

Cylindrical stamps. I shows a braided design combined with shell ornamentation. II uses the same braided pattern, but it is combined with flowers. Both are from Mexico City, National Museum Collections.

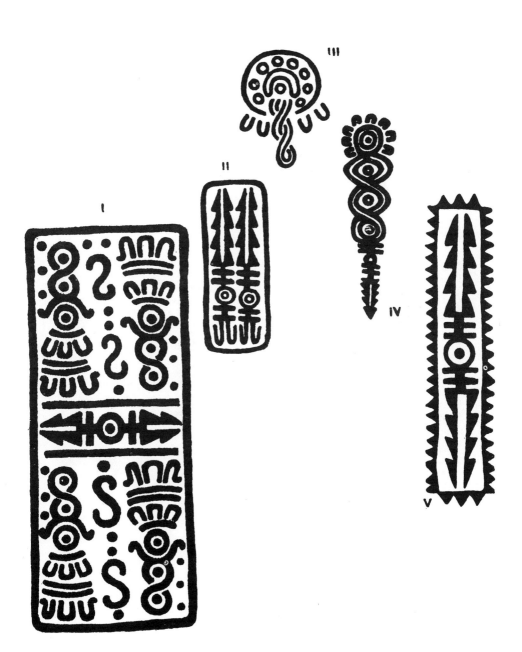

Flat stamps found in Mexico City. The motif is a wooden rattle (Chicahuastli) which was used to mark the rhythm in dances. It is also an attribute of certain gods, priests, and warriors.

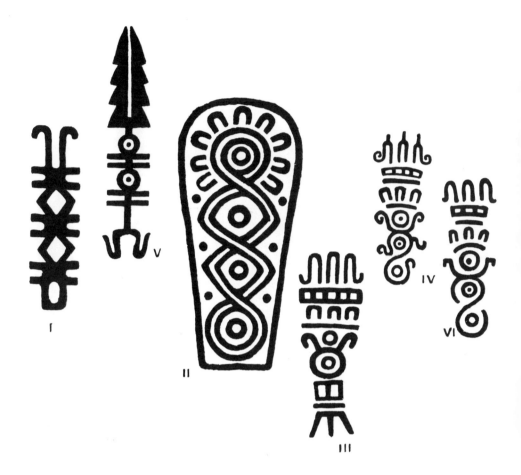

Flat stamps depicting the wooden rattles (Chicahuastli) used in dances, and as an attribute of god, warriors and priests. I and V are from Mexico City. II, III, IV, and VI are from the State of Mexico.

Flat stamps using variations of the wooden rattle (Chicahuastli) pattern, from Mexico City. The rattle was used as a cane by the Fire God, often as a symbol of the priests, and marked the rhythm of the dances.

Flat stamps. I and II show motifs of Patolli, a game similar to Parchesi. III and IV use the same motif and are from Veracruz. I, II, V, and VI are from Mexico City.

Flat stamps depicting movement (Olin). I, II, III, and V are from Mexico City. IV was found in Veracruz.

Flat stamps with various motifs of movement (Olin). I, II, and IV are from Mexico City. VI is from Tenayuca. III, V, and VII are from Mexico. VIII was found in Guerrero.

Flat stamps. The decorations used are architectural elements—turreted wall (Tenamitl), etc. I, II, and VI are from Mexico. III and IV are from Oaxaca. V is from Michoacan.

147

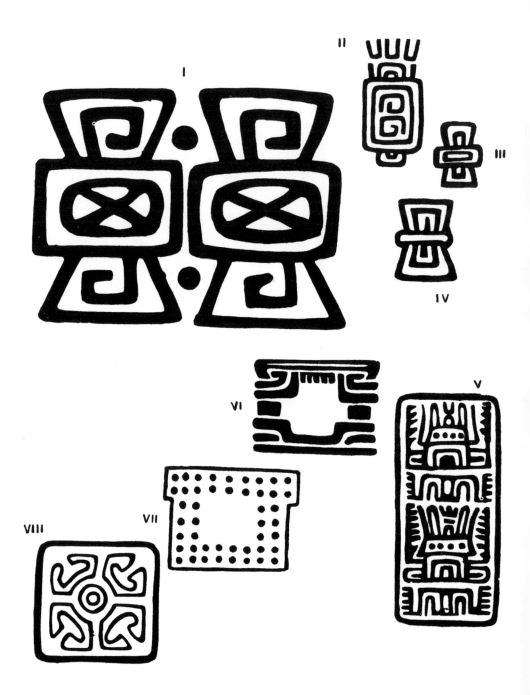

Flat stamps. I, II, III, and IV show motifs of braziers. I and IV are from Mexico City. II is from Yucatan. III is from Mexico. V is not identified and comes from Mexico City. VI represents the Cave of the Earth (Tlalliostoc). VII and VIII are from the State of Mexico, but their patterns have not been identified.

Flat stamps with motifs of trophies. I, II, III, and IV present shields with arrows and flags and were found in Mexico City and Veracruz. IV is in the National Museum Collections.

I

II

III

Flat stamps showing motifs of trophies—lances decorated with blade and floral designs. I is a pheasant. II is a turkey. III is an owl, arrows, and a hand with a shield. All are from Mexico City.

Flat stamps decorated with symbols of the god called Five Flowers (Macuil-xochitl), combined with small shells, butterflies, crosses, etc. All are from the State of Mexico.

151

Flat stamps. I, II, and IV represent the sun emblem. III represents the time emblem. V represents the smoke emblem. I is from Veracruz. II is from Oaxaca. The rest are from Mexico City, National Museum.

Decorative motifs which may have chronological significance. I, possibly indicating the year 1221 or 1225 (Gracia Payon), was found in San Andres Tuxtla. II, III, and IV show important ciphers such as No. 13 and No. 8 and were found in Mexico City. V repeats the same motif but comes from Tabasco.